CW00555772

From this
Street to the Moon

From this Street to the Moon

Nabila Jameel

First published 2021 by Lote Tree Press

www.lotetreepress.com

Paperback ISBN 978-1-9162488-7-8
Hardback ISBN 978-1-9162488-9-2
e-book ISBN 978-1-7398271-0-6

A CIP catalogue record for this book is available from the British Library.

Designed and typeset by Lote Tree Press.

Contents

I

Winter sun and hazy dusk

Billie Jean

Let's catch a plane back to the country
that made us free and taught us laughter, jokes, masti.

We gulped ganna juice until sickly full.
Chilled mangoes were meals in the sticky heat
of monsoon summers: we giggled as the juice trickled
through our fingers down to our feet.

In the winters, freshly roasted peanuts bought
in brown paper bags, from dim-lit shops,
danced, hot in our palms.

We danced to Billie Jean on the table
until the lights went out. We carried candles,
sat on a manji around a lantern, listening to stories
of jinn, witches and the eerie sounds of the gallee.

In the background - the muffled rhythm,
the soft music, still audible, of your father's poetry.

masti: messing around
ganna: sugar cane
manji: wooden bed with base of hand-braided natural rope
gallee: street

Roti

How deftly her hands start a fire:
wafting smoke with cardboard.
She blows in rhythms. Rolling pin,
flour, dough: all seated beside her.

Her hands look used: the skin is tough and brown.
She sits, crouched on a small stool, smiling at me.
I see the alert whites of her eyes.
The burning wood crackles.
The bricks around the feisty fire seat a hot pan.
There is promise of a meal.

(My thoughts drift to our little kitchen back home:
the white gas cooker is dull and my mother wears an apron.
I only ever see this much sparkle on Bonfire night;
even then our hands are gloved).

Dusted flour tips over the edge, filling my lungs.
The roti inflates, mimicking the moon.
I look up. We have stars for spotlights.
She signals at me to keep the roti covered.

I wrap the last one: forcing a stream of steam
through the cloth. The fire dies
a naturally timed death. My cousin scoops
the utensils straight into the nook of his elbow.

We step into a lantern-lit room, full of hungry relatives

and chatter. We sit, cross-legged, on a yellow straw mat,
eat with our bare hands from mismatched plates.
I look at my aunt: there is flour in her hair.

The Tailor

Six of his workers with Singer machines
are squeezed into this cavern of rainbow

streams. Thread and cloth of every delight
exciting the nimble fingers of these men

draw the women in. They bring in bags
of black and red lace, organza and chiffon,

satin and silk, ready for the measuring tape.
He looks forward to taking statistics:

bust, waist, hips. It's the closest he gets
to a woman. Rushing the grey-haired ones,

he has his eyes on the younger beauties
with pert breasts and mascara-flushed

inviting eyes, fluttering
in a queue under the tired fan.

Sugar Cane

We chew it like animals in the wild,
spitting the dry chunks of straw-like strands
into a bowl between us.

Our throats dry from July's heat
soften and moisten with every drop.

Not even our shadows on the wall care
that we're sticky and wet –
innocence projected by lanterns.

Starching

She empties the rice into a colander,
collects the water in a bowl, lets it cool.
The wash area is a tap, a hosepipe, a bowl and a drain.

We sit on stools made of woven nylon.
She soaks the cotton shalwar kameez
in the milky bowl swirling it with her brown hands,
then squeezing it; I see her discoloured and brittle fingernails.
The clothes look sticky; the starch looks like
wallpaper paste pooling onto the blue mosaic tiles beneath us.

She then rinses the garments three times under the tap.
We hang them up to dry in February's breeze
and then sit inside so that I can smooth her hands
with whatever I can find: a forgotten bottle of Nivea cream.

Chaand Raat

~ Night of the new moon ~

Twinkling, glistening,
they soften the tube lights.
Tilted boxes are treasures displayed
to the approaching footsteps of teenage girls.

Bare fragile arms advance over counters of glass
into the silent hands of men, to be checked for size.
The girls choose the colours from a gallery
of crimson, magenta, green, hot pink and black rings.

There are numerous shades of every colour,
from ready red to broody beige. Subdued aisles
of careful conversations are eclipsed with excitement
at the thought of the first kiss of the wrist.

He takes her hand in his, squeezing her thumb and little finger
until they meet and her hand disappears in to his.
She recoils with discomfort, staring at his face as he slips
the bangles, one by one onto her hand, sliding them along,
with short thrusts, towards the wrist.

She shrieks with an unexpected cut
and begins to cry –
he catches her blood with a hasty tissue.
Wiping the droplets from his hands,
he glances at the frowning mother.

17

Paratha

The true paratha is layered
like generations of our mothers.

Authenticity is in the rolls and folds
of aata, fattened with ghee.

Dusted and rolled out like puff pastry
it becomes an ordinary looking roti.

No utensil is used to turn the sizzling
paratha over; fingers are accustomed

to heat and the spit of excited butter.
Hot on your plate you tear it

in hunger's haste and dip it
in sweetened yoghurt.

The true paratha is layered
like generations of our mothers.

aata: chapatti flour

Bank of Bra

She wipes her face with the end
of her dupatta, signs to him, to wait.

Pushing her left boob up with her left hand,
she roughly burrows into the bra with her right,

pulls out two Ten Rupee notes -
folded and flattened with sweat.

The notes gasp with fresh air.
She slaps his palm with the money

like a bloke laying cards on the table
and walks off with her bag of groceries.

Taanga

~ horse and carriage ~

Clattering clogs I think of, as I lean over to see the horse's hooves,
scared of becoming mash under the wheels of the taanga.

My mother, my aunt and I are pressed into this bony carriage
of leather coverings, rusting metal and weeping wood.

There is even a mirror at either side: I make funny faces in it.
The sun catches my eye and watches my mischief.

Holding the metal handle at the side, I close my eyes
and let the warm air clothe my hair. The horse bells jingle.

I look down and see happy flies on dark brown, wet dung,
freshly laid in a trail by our beautifully decorated horse.

taanga: horse carriage

'Ber'

~ Pakistani jujube (pronounced 'bear') ~

They are like grapes, but larger, chunkier, crunchier.
Some green, some pale, some red.
I take one and bite it.
It's like apple, mixed with pear.
Where did you get these from?

Let me show you, you say.
We all walk up the path,
under the hanging branches of limp trees.
You ask us to slow down outside a posh house,
looking around shiftily. A Vespa stutters past
and then a rikshaw, heavy with loud women.

A tired cow with arched skin under its ribs
walks up to us, staring at us with suspicious eyes.
I sense we are about to do something wrong.
You laugh and sprint up the trunk,
hands and feet working like a chimp's.
I want to climb too but am scared of falling
or my shalwar slipping off.

The string under your kurta dangles
as you stretch one arm to pull a handful of bear.
We giggle and look away.
The whole branch shakes!
Within seconds, it's *raining bears.*

Jamadarni

~ toilet cleaner ~

I hear her sandals sweep
the cold concrete floor.

It takes her just ten minutes
to scoop clean

the five Roman style toilets. She leaves
with a large bag that hangs like a full bowel

in her hand. In the other, a ten rupee note
which quickly folds into her small bosom.

Billo

His large plump lips
framed with fresh stubble
are painted with the reddest red
like the walls of these garish shops.

The plait is flung to the side
over his grisly chest. Peering through
the polyester kameez is a padded bra,
unevenly stuffed.

He stops to flirt with the ganna-juice man
who gives him a free pint glass
of sweet froth. It is load-shedding time -
the shops switch off with a buzz.

Billo is heard laughing loud to which
sparks from the cigarette lighters dazzle.
The heavy jangle of his anklets
fuses with his Bata sandals.

ganna: sugar cane

Muli ki Roti

~ Roti of radish ~

The silver pots and pans are laid out on the flat roof.
We help to peel and grate the muli.
It is so large, I cannot control its movements:
like a man on stilts it wobbles.

There is no such radish in England.
Like potato, it oozes bubbly starch.
We squeeze the mass of flakes, then add all the spices
while our aunt makes the dough. In goes the coriander.

She makes dough balls, then rolls them one by one,
filling them with muli. Buttered, the roti sizzles in the pan
until crisp on both sides. The smell invites the crows
aligned on the tallest brick wall behind us.

We eat in the sun. Too full to move,
we guzzle bottles of cold Sprite.
Later, in and out of a snooze, I watch the crows
have a party of their own.

Suitcases in a Wheelbarrow

The van won't squeeze down this winding
village street. There's a resting cow,
woken up from its snooze,
staring at all the commotion.

It's like a clip from Faulty Towers,
order within chaos, and a little luck.

Our suitcases need to be taken up
the street to the van for our long
journey to Lahore.

To avoid several trips up and down
this vein of a street, a wheelbarrow
is ordered, arriving without delay.

The cow is now up on its wobbly legs
and standing closer.

A dark and rickety man is in charge.
He lifts each suitcase carefully, gently
placing all of them, one by one,
into the wheelbarrow.

A task so perfectly done, with all
its imperfections, assuredly, confidently,
with a let's-not-waste-time-faffing-about approach.
All our luggage is in our wheelbarrow.

We try to gulp down our laughter.
Giggling like girls, we say goodbye
and step into the van, bracing ourselves
for the pothole and ditch peppered

rocky road to Lahore.

Day Long Siesta

Sosan steals straw mats from her begum sahiba's
drawing room while she is busy on the phone with a friend.
(The mats are sold to the man on the street six miles away
who says things from England are worth gold).

Her starved body looks for scraps.
Begum sahiba throws leftovers from last night's party
into a thin black 'shopper' and thrusts it at her
with rolling eyes, relieved it cleared the space for more.

The rat is disappointed that night to find nothing
in the window of the high-rise flat. Smelling crumbs,
it scuttles to begum sahiba's cotton wool separated toes,
that twitch in sync with her snores.

Nowshera

7.30 am: stood in the school grounds,
I wish I had learnt the national anthem.
Miming the words with little grace,
my throat clams up, sweaty palms grip my bag.
My back is straight and obedient and my fingernails
dig into my own palms with nervous pulse.
I don't know *what* we are chanting.

My throat is as dry as the unwelcoming earth
beneath my new khussey. Noreen smiles at me,
exaggerating her lip movements so I can follow.
She is only six and understands
that her teacher needs guiding.

The Pathan cook makes his own music
in the cubicle of a kitchen, unfit for cooking.
He sings in Pashto from under his turban.
He is the only Pathan I hear laughing.

I know the ordeal is over when the sun is higher.
Noreen takes my hand, looking up at me
grinning with her bright green eyes:
eyes that remind me of English fields.

I loosen my fist and smile at her.
We leave the grounds in single file,
smooth as the sly snakes in the harsh grass
of our boundaries.

I see the cool classrooms - converted caves
of this colonial remnant. Sensing the headteacher's
eyes on me, I turn to look: she swings her keys playfully.
Three of the teachers giggle. I read their lips: 'Farangi'.

khussey: delicate and traditional leather shoes, often embroidered
farangi: foreigner

Saturday in Hayatabad

I travelled 50 miles in a Hiace
packed with workers
browned by the ruthless sun.
They gazed at me. I pulled the shawl
over my head , shoulders and arms.

A taxi took me to Main Bazaar.
Women in black burkey
haggled with tired,
irate shopkeepers.
Roadside stalls of sweetcorn,
Peshawari naan and chapli kebabs
didn't tempt me.

In a long queue outside
'Shahid's Imported goods'
I waited for half an hour,
sweat tickling my spine;
mouth wet for bland food.

Inside, the cold blast of air
from the air con made me shiver.
Imperial Leather, Lux and Palmolive
shampoo were passed from hand
to hand until it reached the woman
with a cockney accent, her voice
gleaming among the Pathaans.

Then it was my turn:
I asked for five tins of baked beans
in my northern, rustic accent.

burkey: plural of burka

Pathaans: originating from NWFP in Pakistan

Bahria Town – 'modernisation'

It has a desi grace, flashing
its dizzying neon lights of red and blue,
almost like a preening bird,
that also reminds me of the airmail letters
dropping through the letterbox of my childhood.

'Here's our Eiffel Tower!'
the two wide-eyed teens exclaim,
searching for the same delight in our eyes.

'Er-yes, very nice. Bohat khub *(wonderful)!*
Wah!' we reply.

I feel sad as we walk around this imitation,
and listen to the teens talk in American-inflected speech,
as they show off what their country has to offer.

After a coffee and a doughnut,
served by smiling staff,
in a clean café, we say goodbye
and drive back, rolling the windows down,

to breathe in the grit, dirt,
beeping madness and dust.
We are brimming with lust to tuck
into Lahori life under the dusky sky,
just one more time, like a last kiss,
before we depart.

Linguistic Map.

You can change your Pound Sterling
at Ravi Money Exchange, then drive
down to Shami road, via Charing Cross
and on the way you'll see Ganga Ram Hospital.

There are many Chemists and Druggists here
and on the way to the hustling bustling embroidery
cluster, you'll see The Medicators.

In the clothes shop, to try on for size,
you go to the *Try Room,*
and if you need the loo, don't ask
for the *bathroom,* the *ladies*
or the *toilet,* simply ask
for the *washroom.*

Houses Speak

Sentences scream out
from books as we unbolt the door.
The library is a hardback history book,
when opened - an exhibition of ageing paper,
so fragile, that if touched, words crumble and spill.
The reading chairs are facing one another,
in meeting mode – they have been talking
for fifteen years.

Pots and pans, cups and plates, wake up,
waiting to be moved, like children too small to get up.
They've been holding warm chatter, now clay cold.

Like a neglected old lady
without a carer to comb her hair,
disabled with age,
everything from table to chair,
to picture frame, needs to be cleaned,
propped up, repositioned.

The crack in the cold, damp wall
is heartache visualised, an artery
from the ceiling to the floor,
about to give way to a major collapse.

Beds are numb and paralysed.
Photographs of deceased forefathers
encased in glass-fronted cupboards

still have a pulse - their eyes connect
with ours for a few moments
as they lean into the room.

In the courtyard I hear water dripping
somewhere – a slow release of the soul
of the house as it takes its last breaths.

Jhelum

I

Legend has it that Alexander the Great's
horse Jhelum died here and so the city
was named after it.

It is believed that Jhelum signifies
the 'hoof mark' in Greek and that the horse
left a mark on the soft ground on this spot.

Legend also delivers the myth that
Jhelum is a compound of two Greek words:
'Jul' and 'Hum' ('cool' 'water').

II

Jhelum also means I'm wild and free, filled with love
to the brim, about to burst; aunties and cousins,
winter sun and hazy dusk; playing chase around a well,
splashing in the courtyard, drenched by the cooling rain;
everyone laughing at me for the way I talk and act
but loving me all the same.

It means sweet juicy mangoes squishing in our hands,
biting into chunks of chilling sugar cane; excitedly running
up to the roof, then leaning over to watch processions of goats;
watching a healthy goat being slaughtered, its blood gushing
into the drain; long goodbyes and sobbing until you're back on
the plane.

III

Jhelum also means the crumbling of an empire
and the slow struggles of a civilisation,
the haunting shadows of colonial buildings,
ghostly, grey, grim;

independence, with dependence,
poverty and posh kothees,
starving faces, begging amputees;

love stories, long distance calls,
the inky stamp on the letter addressed
to a terraced house in a small English town,
excitedly opened by a millworker's hands.

IV

Welcoming coffins to the homeland.
It's where it begins and ends, at the hoof-mark
of Alexander the Great's horse.

kothees: villas

II

England is a jazeera, an island!

Look! Snow!

Her hair is darker and silkier than the satin sky.
Her husband takes her hand. She balances,
like a child learning to walk. The baby wriggles
inside her, its head nestled, lungs growing for icy air.

With the other hand she takes a clump of snow,
glittering at the bottom of the window.
Her palm invites the new sensation.
Under her tenuous steps, it crunches.

The glow of a distant street lamp reveals a passer-by
who tips his cap and smiles at them both,
her fascination endearing. They wave.
She shudders, with snow crackling in her mouth.

Passport

~ For my father ~

He has the scent of loyalty,
when he comes home tired,
hands the crispy wage packet to mum,
eats in haste and falls asleep as if he's drugged.
He smells of dust - I know this is the smell of work.

On his day off he wears a crisp shirt,
stretches his tired legs and sometimes mutters to himself.
I think he cries too. I think he misses
daada and daadi, whom I've never met.

We gather around him
like cubs to hear the same stories
about his childhood over and over again.
Each time they sound new because
he has magic in his voice.
He is a magnificent library.

My sisters and I get to rub
baby talc onto his chest.
We laugh when all the hairs turn white.
We paint his nails pink; our dad is a clown!
We laugh until our tummies ache.
He cuddles up to my mum
like a bear: it's the only time he's human.

daada / daadi: paternal father/mother

Blackpool

Our parents took us every summer.
Five of us packed in the back
of the Cortina without seatbelts.
Dad: wearing a well pressed shirt,
mum: bride-like, adorned with gold.

At the Pleasure Beach,
we had a few gentle rides
that wouldn't risk death
but were uncertain enough
to slightly dislodge our hearts.

Then we'd find a bench, sit down
and have fish and chips, the wind coating
our faces with salty air; then a walk
on the beach, with bags of candy floss
ballooning from my sister's pram,

mimicking my mother's inflated
shalwar under her embroidered kameez.
We were lined up in age order so dad
could take photos with his new camera –
soon to fill our family album, in which

there was only us. Photos of this 'exotic place'
were sent to relatives in Pakistan; photos,
that captured a temporary joy, a one-day holiday,
away from our permanent existence.

Swastika

He stuck it on her back
while she was choosing bananas.
I pulled it off –
he slapped my hand
and put it back on.

She turned around.
Others looked on.
He stood back and watched
as she silently paid for the fruit.
I whispered to her.

She took off her coat,
removed the sticker, while inspecting it.
The punk sniggered;
his eyes, a sharp blue, brightened.

Others looked on as she swung the pushchair
full of shopping into his legs and fouled
through the mouth in Panjabi:
our fierce tongue that shredded
fear and intimidation, through its own
fear and intimidation of 'foreignness'.

Her voice thundered through
the music playing in the shopping centre,
smashing every syllable of silence
in passers-by, stunning them into stillness.

The punk ran away, as pale as a cabbage.
My legs trembled, her body hot with anger.

To this day I remember that cold clammy
hand grabbing my wrist; I remember
looking at NF graffiti and learning
the phonics for hatred.

The Sewing Machinist

-for my mother -

We're always woken by the heavy and loud
humdrum of the Singer machine and there is always
a carpet of thread to walk over.

I often wonder why it's called *Singer* –
there's nothing melodious about the noise
reverberating through every wall and floorboard.

We don't complain, although we hate it,
because we know that's where new clothes
and PIA tickets come from;

Mum sews and sews…
to stuff the mouths of those greedy suitcases
with presents she can't afford.

She sews and sews…
stitches for new gold earrings,
our days out to Blackpool or the zoo.

The head seamstress who lives two streets away
sends us heavy bundles of fabric with a deadline of a week.

The bundles land on our living room floor
blowing cotton that sticks to every surface,
including our skin and hair, clogging the arteries of our house.

Mum sits with a cup of tea which she either never finishes
or gulps down piping hot.

Then she analyses the anatomy of a denim jacket.
I watch her sew the pockets on for the next three hours.

In that time I tend to my brother, my eye on the bundle
of pockets that reduces slowly until the carpet is visible.

But she carries on.

Her hair as chaotic as the thread on the floor,
her face tired, too anxious to look away
in case a penny-shaped second is lost.

Copper Coins

Copper coins filled the China Green tea tin to the brim
which sat in the nook of the Victorian chest.

Every afternoon the tin was emptied by tiny hands
for Curly Wurlys, Potato Puffs and Hubba Bubbas
from the shop next door.

He'd come home tired with more copper coins.
As his taxi cooled, he filled the tin.

The Old Man with the Dog

Sees me getting off the bus and speeds up,
unleashing his dog:

Get the paki! Go on! Get the paki!

The dog barks and chases me.
I sprint like I've never done before.
My heart explodes and my chest hurts,
my legs go numb and I fall.

What's the matter love?
It's only a dog!

He pulls his licking dog away

Paki! he sniggers and spits near me
then walks away,
humming to himself.

A Book Closer to Home.

Every Saturday mum took us to the library.
We dispersed into different parts of the room,

craving this yellow smell of bound paper
and a peep into lives we did not live -
where tea was not chai, but dinner.

Mum sat in the Urdu section,
soon dissolving into a magazine
full of squiggles that only made sense to her.

Her large almond eyes smiled.
Her soft fingers turned the pages,
pausing while she glanced at us with motherly duty.

We sat with our books on the carpeted floor,
following the curves and lines of English
with our fingertips,

the red signs on the mahogany shelves
silencing our tongues.

The Island in Preston

I remember this in the middle
of a busy junction, being breathless
as we ran up and down it
on our way to town.

The grass was like carpet –
we wondered if it was real.
The sun was warmer on our faces
at the top of this island.

We would talk about it
with our cousins in Pakistan.
They said to us 'but you live on an island;
England is a jazeera, an island!'

I see it now - levelled ground,
holding a Care Home. Through windows
I see sullen faces waiting for death,
that once smiled at our innocence,
when we plucked daisies
at the top of our island.

School Bus

Fat ginger kid breathes heavily.
He has no friends and sits alone on the bus.
He's ready with a mouth of spit.
With projectile thrust and perfect aim he spits
at a terrified eleven year old in pigtails
just as she's getting off the bus.
She runs home, shaking, tears like acid
burning her face in the icy wind.

She gets inside and runs upstairs, scrubs
green phlegm and spit before her parents
suspect anything. Her father cannot know –
he has sent her three miles away to a white school,
aiming for the best education and social mobility.
White is *better*, just like moving out of an Asian area
is *better*; if only it didn't cost going through hell each day.

Factory Worker's Day Off

He unwinds on a Saturday morning
in a fresh shirt, hair glistening.
She washes the breakfast dishes,
silently enjoying his presence.

The radiogram takes up half a wall:
bulky upper body, standing on skinny
teak legs, thumping heavily through
the discoloured wallpaper.

Sitting back on the sofa, he stretches
his feet from the week's taxi-ing.

He hums…

ta ra ram pam pam
ta ra ram pam pam

Asha, Kishore, Lata, Mehdi, Rafi
can be heard bellowing from the chimney tops.

Our Front Room

Rarely filled with guests -
sofa backs, shiny cushions
never shifted out of place;

but it was our disco on Saturday nights.
Fluorescent tube lights and Blackburn Radio
made our faces glow like the two-bar
heater in the corner.

Mum would close the door
so my baby sis wouldn't wake,
fling off her dupatta,
turn the volume up loud.

My mum was a teenager!
I, her dancing partner!
(My dad's feet were over-timing,
tapping the pedals of his taxi-ing Cortina).

Her limbs crudely
imitated Hema Malini.
Hot and sweaty from punching
and kicking the air –

my mum: a reddish brown,
me: a pinky olive.
Two amateurs, delirious
on a domestic stage.

Talcum Powder

Like cubs, the three of us curl up around you
and on your lap, coated with the smell
of talc from your chest.

One by one we take a handful
of hair and pull until you playfully shriek 'ouch!'
'Pull out the white ones' you say -

so we pluck and pull,
watching the discomfort
in your scrunched up face.
        We laugh.

We dust your chest with more talc,
as if it were a cake.

Now the memory spills out,
like icing, onto this page.

Surma

~ kohl ~

An old ornate bottle
covered in a metal lattice
of flowers, sat on our mahogany
dressing table for as long as I can remember.

Mum would shake the bottle,
pull out the stopper
and swipe my eyes
with cold thick kohl,
turning them into those
of a *'hirni'*(a deer).

Then she would mark my cheek
with a dot, to remove *nazar* –
the evil eye of admiration.

Back Yard

Every summer
on a Saturday morning
you bathed us in the back yard
of our terraced house on St. George's Road.

We had pink Lux, a bucket, a sponge and a jug.
The sun would dry the suds on our skin
that would stick like icing and make us white.
Bubbles were bigger than our house.

You rinsed us and then we were brown again.
We sat towel wrapped in the sun
and shivered while droplets fell onto our flip flops.
Smiles were bigger than our house.

Phonetics Seminar

Jones has given me an E
for an essay on *Intonation*.
Everyone else has passed.
Everyone else is white.

I noticed in the introductory lesson
she wiped her hands on her back
after accidentally brushing mine
when giving handouts.

But, as usual, I brushed it off as me being
over-sensitive, just like when at college
I was told by a pleasantly surprised teacher:
you're very articulate as an Asian!

My ears may not be trained well yet
to listen out for the slight nuances
in a newsreader's speech,
but my eyes don't miss anything.

I stare at the grade all morning,
my stomach burning,
my heart pounding.

I storm out at break,
to the office,
my palms sweating,
my stomach tight.

When I am given a C
I realise I have won my first battle.
Jones never undermarks me again.

Morning Orchestra

I know you're downstairs
when I'm woken by the merciless
beating of an egg. There's warmth
and comfort in this noise.

There's a perfectly timed
gap between each beat -
despite your crippling arthritis,
your wrist works in unison,
musically, lyrically.

Not a single drop spills
even though you tilt the bowl
to help you whip the egg into foam.
The egg goes straight into the pan
of browned onions, announcing a loud
splatter and sizzle.

There's no omelette without drama, of course.
There's no soul in the kitchen without dad.

Ideology

From my living room window I see the dad opposite
holding his new-born who's dressed in a Union Jack baby grow.

The family is cheering Griffin.

There's a pile of BNP leaflets in my porch -
they've been dropping through my letterbox all week.

That same night I'm woken by a helicopter.
The next day I read about the victim

of a vicious knife attack; the fate of a law-abiding
citizen walking home from the mosque.

If glue could fix everything

Becoming Medusa

One day, in a rage, I chop my greasy plait,
throw it under the bed, shake my head and stare
in the mirror, flushed with anger and regret.

I look like Medusa. It's a mess. I cry.
Then I look again: ugly but empowered.
Every strand hisses at the myth of womanhood:

'a woman's beauty is in her hair'.

Now I will burn in hell, with no hair to cover
my breasts on the day of judgement.
My changing shape is a curse -

a curse that stops me from riding a bike
or skipping in the street as I'm pulled inside
by a panicked mother who hands me a dupatta,

eager to guard my chastity. The battle
to wear jeans makes me a man for some reason,
to wear make-up implies a loss of virginity.

dupatta: a long scarf that drapes over the shoulders and chest

Arranged

The conservatory in our house
is the perfect place for dad to place us,
like dolls on the mantelpiece,
ensuring there's no hanky-panky
with a boy if there's any chemistry.

He divides us from him to provide
a safe space for us to talk, private enough
to sound proof our physical voices
but exposed enough to see our inner thoughts.

The furniture has been arranged
according to the laws of comfortable distance,
so elbows or knees don't converse.
We are in our shrouds of respectability:
not too tight, not too short, plenty of gold.

Dad places himself on the edge of the sofa,
unaware that I can hear and feel his every move.
I peep into his head and see myself
in wedding gown again.
He sees it as red. I see it as black.

My sisters have sat here.
I have sat here.
The mediocre conversations
have dissolved into the brick here.
Samosey and Rubicon. Biscuits and tea.

We are drained from the ritualistic
gestures of hospitality.

When the family leaves, we relax,
like over-inflated balloons ready to pop.
In the coming days and weeks
we await an *offer* or *rejection*
from the boy's family.

Rules for the Bride

Don't look up.
Keep head lowered.
Fold yourself inwards like
the *mimosa pudica,*
recoiling from the slightest touch.

Don't look at the groom
but catch the occasional glance
when you think no one is looking.
Don't smile.
Don't laugh.
Sit still.
Wait to be spoken to.

Open your red bud mouth
to the *orchis* sized laddu.
But swallow elegantly,
be ladylike.
Catch the crumbs.

Sob uncontrollably when
you're escorted to the car.
Think morbid thoughts:
someone who died,
someone who hurt you.
Cry until your face is a palette
of spilled black ink.

Proposal 13

Time for her to go down now and look bashful but sexy.
Proposal 13 comes in and makes himself comfy -
doesn't look much at the young divorcee.
She's not a virgin, he's thinking, then again neither is he.
She still looks deliciously sweet.
How many has *he* slept with? How much more can he eat?

Father steps out and 13 undresses her with his eyes.
She knows her fate and wants to say
how much she hates his style.
He asks her *can you cook and how many kids do you want?*
He tells her, *mum needs care and I work away a lot.*
She asks him *have you fathered a child illegitimately?*
Tell me how many women have you made divorcees?

He chokes and laughs and father enters
whose ear was glued to the wall.

Thank you for having me, Mr Rashid.
   -   *I'll give you another call.*

Reply to a Marriage Proposal

Take me not as your property,
a new acquisition, a shining asset,
but a dilapidated outbuilding
that you stumble across,
requiring care and attention.

You see its history of lives lived
on all the walls and in the streaks
on the window. Even the sun's rays
dim as they hit the rooftop.

Display

In public,
he is always the *zabbar (a)*
    she the *zeyr (e)*

In private,
they can hold hands like a *hyphen.*

'He is a Station Above Her'

In those slow mornings,
when the sky turns pink,

and she's sipping tea,
still heavy eyed with sleep,

he can't help himself
but pull the duvet away

to uncover her waking toes.
He takes her foot in his hand,

stroking it, firmly kissing the sole,
making her giggle.

His morning worship,
at her feet, complete.

If Glue Could Fix Everything.

Returning to the table
she sighs at the empty space
hearing the cutlery tinker
between his fingers
and clatter on the plate.

Placing a vase of lilies on the ring,
she wishes he had used coasters.
She ties the Bamboo knives and forks
and places them in a drawer
for things labelled 'unsure'.

She wipes away his smile
with salt from her eyes
mixed with a spray of Pledge.
Tomorrow she will buy some varnish
and fix that loosened leg.

Convenience

Their local mini-market.
The chip shop.
The post office.

The bed they share
for the crescent moon smile
of their child.

Sirens

She stinks of spit, holding her burning wrist.
The bed is still on its side.
Two officers make notes and sigh.

The crater in the wall is examined close up.
Plasterboard crumbles onto ceramic shards
of the shattered 'Circle of Love'.

She picks glass from the soles of her feet.
In the corner, standing in a puddle of urine,
her toddler incessantly cries.

Gamble

There, by the bookshelf,
he trapped her in the corner,
tickled her until she was breathless.

There, by the sink, he caught her,
kissed her exposed shoulder,
slowing the morning rush.

There, at the table, he threw
the plate that hit the shoulder
he kissed that very morning.

Falling in Love

The earth loses momentum
and the sky bows to the seas

when I'm lost
in the planets of your eyes.

Falling out of Love

Gulping his laughter he says:

'Babe, I'm gonna light
your degree certificate with a match'

to which all the mates laugh.

She is silent, her smile wiped
like abruptly smudged lipstick.

It is then, in that moment that

    she falls,

with a blow to the head and heart,

      tumbling

       down

         a long staircase

of dreams and promises.

It is then,

        in that moment,

          that she

  falls

    several steps

out of love.

Unrequited

In the tight clasp
of his coffee cup,

in the spaces between
the words he utters,

in the mirror that catches
three seconds of love,

to which she is oblivious.
She talks, she talks.

He listens, smiling,
loving in silence the gold

in her night sky hair
catching the lamp light,

the way her eyes ignite
when she says another's name.

My Best Friend

You absorb it all, this toxic fury,
never judge me, soak up all my ramblings
of hot ink. If I don't sit with you,
I become pale, withdrawn,
heavy with routine's monotone.

In a room of silence,
you've seen me cry,
felt all my tremors,
grabbed my hand, just in time,
when I'm about to drift into sadness.

In odd hours, 2 am, 4 am,
I'm jolted out of sleep from
wherever I've travelled to,
lines buzzing in my head.
You catch my vibrant dreams.

When I drift away, mid-conversation,
among mediocre people, you turn up again
listen to me talk endlessly about things that matter.

Only you see me at my most disgraceful –
hissing and spitting words,
which I later cross out, apologetically.
I use you, waste you, sheet after sheet
of illegible scrawling, scrunch you
in my hands in a finale,

until something sensical emerges.
Something that looks like a poem.

Sometimes I leave you for months,
picking you up again –
you nurture me into something
most elegant and graceful.

Blank page, my friend,
you're wonderful.

Life in Boxes

~ in the name of hope ~

We sleep on the make-shift bed:
two parts of a sofa joined like two Lego bricks,
and through the window floods in moonlight –
pure, crystal, white. I've lost count
of the times I've *started a new life.*
There's no gas, no heat,
nothing to cook on or with

but we have two brand new
Costa cups waiting to be opened.

In the living room lie our futures,
anxious, distressed, tangled,
dusting off distrust and demons.
A few boxes lie half open, with our lives
spilling out, heavy and thick.
Even those boxes are tired of carrying our weight;
patched up with extra strong tape at the base.

The large box that holds us both is this house
and it smells of the last tenant's troubles:
curtain poles hungover, carpet worn to its bones,
bathroom odour, hair in the drain,
layers of dust on windowsills.

but we have two brand new
Costa cups waiting to be opened.

Ostracised

She sees the seasons peel away the scene
from snow that sends beams into the sky
to blossom that kisses the pavement pink.

She sees the weather fade the kindness of kin
until she can't think of a name for 'next of kin'
in capital bold ink.

She's a pothole avoided, an empty bench,
a revolving door, a faithful tree that never moves.
Something only peripherally present.

Unreported

Volcanic heat plunges up her body,
making her evening lipstick crimson,
her chest thud, moving her to him
until she's stood in confrontation.

She hints that she knows his filthy secret.
She watches the colour fade from his face.
In her head she imagines him being whipped,
beaten and tortured. Then left to die in a cell.

But she makes conversation, with the occasional
sharp pin stab of a word to unnerve him,
violently shifting the plush carpet from under his feet.
Is this how he pulled down the pants of small boys?

The next day she speeds to the station where justice
for children awaits. She stops her car, tears streaming
down her face, handcuffed by the biggest bastard
of all criminals: that word *izzat*.

izzat: honour

Blood is (not) Thicker than Water

We wait to be called from by those we expect from.
We're pleasantly surprised when we hear from those
we *don't* expect anything from.

We can build an entire family of friends, develop
that strange telepathic bond when one is thinking
of the other, the other calls and your heart skips a beat.

We can laugh or cry, tell our deepest
secrets and fears to those bloodless connections:
and we will never be damned or judged.

Mother

They are from you, of you
but are not *you.*

They arrive through you;
you're a very long wait at a bus stop

until they reach their destination,
leaving you weaker and worn.

Now you feel like your life has begun,
but menopause hits you

and the pain of childbirth seems
like a wasp sting in comparison.

You slow down, cook meals for two.
You become a revolving door,

for them to come and go,
often when they're in trouble.

Then one day you hold their children,
doubling your heart in size.

That bus stop turns into a train station,
complete with car park.

The cycle repeats:

You're cooking in large pots
and tripping over Lego bricks.

Visiting Time

An amoeba-shaped stain
on the bleached sheet
beneath your swollen thighs
increases in size.

The curtains enclose you. The midwife,
whose hands you know so well,
helps to latch your new-born to your
burning breast.

With each suck, your womb contracts.
You cry. She thinks you're in pain,
passing you a pain-killer
on a surgical silver tray.

You do not hear your child,
only the cooing voices
of fathers, in Ward 5.

Daughter

I, a small three and a half,
you have outgrown me – a size six.
Now you pinch clothes from my wardrobe
yet the trouser length does not fit.

So you gather it all around the hips
with a belt glowing with 'High School Musical'
in pink. Mascara is a bit too much which hides
your innocence. Lips- lips which shimmer,

over glossed: I see that I am losing my grip.
It only seems like yesterday when you were
a bundle of six pounds and six. You look at me,
not up to me. Our eyes meet like a spirit level.

Soon you will be five foot six as I get close
to forty and shrink. You no longer hold my hand
or run to me for a hug. Instead you walk closely,
holding your mobile for love.

Son

You undress in front of me
as if you're still five,

as if I'm a mirror.
I need to look away –

you're no longer a boy,
but my curiosity makes me look

at the soft virginal hairs on your legs
catching the light from the window.

Your shoulders are broadening.
Your back is strong.

Your hands are manly.
You could lift me.

I step out of the room,
close the door and crave

the clam-like soft baby
that slept on my chest,

when my fragile arms
were once your shell.

31st October

I am burying my daughter's pre-molars
in the back garden. With her swollen mouth,
she mumbles, 'mummy, the neighbours
will think you killed someone.' I look around –
only the plants seem bemused;
they almost twitch with discomfort.

My son steps out in his Ben 10 wellies
hovers over my shoulder, agitated,
with an unused purple spade in his dimpled grip.
We dig deep and move the sleeping baby bulbs.
He asks about the tooth fairy and witches
as we cover the little pit of disturbed English worms
wriggling around the blood stained packet.
I place 10p in his soiled palm, let him believe in fairies
and tell him that we hid the tooth from the witch –
we call that witch a *jinn*.

Later that night we answer the door
to trick or treating horrors; he places five Chupa Chups
in their curled, innocent palms with his tiny sticky fingers.

Grandson

I

I am surveying the windows and doors
of the house, with a bottle of Windolene
in one hand, cloth in the other.
I leave one glass square that is smeared
with your chubby handprints.

The square frames your fascination
with the cat that sits opposite, on the shed roof.
I can hear you call out to her: 'woof woof!'
as you turn to me intermittently,
wide-eyed with wonder.

There is a story encased in this frame of PVC,
including your first words with the angry wind,
the slashing rain and cushioning snow.

II

Your left hand emerges like a crane,
with unrefined robotic mobility,
while your right hand rests on your lap.

The hand moves towards the plate
of finely chopped fruit. The fingers
clumsily co-ordinate the pick-up

of a quartered grape.

The forefinger and thumb work together,
hastily lifting the small morsel towards the mouth -
like a rocket-ship taking off, or a starved eagle
with prey in mouth, ready to fly.

I watch, slightly amused,
holding my hands to let you learn.

Your fingers lose grip and the quartered grape
comes tumbling down your chest, like a rock falling
under nature's force on a cliff edge. Your mouth closes
as abruptly as a shutter, your face creases in disappointment.

I watch, slightly amused,
holding my hands to let you learn.

Finally, a second attempt later,
the battered and bruised grape
is slushing around in your tiny mouth,
your four milky teeth sparkling in glory,
while your triumphant eyes shout:
        'I did it, Nano!'

The Shaded Area

She may not be the mother but there she is, nevertheless.
She stands, to one side, like a forgotten ornament

in a glass cabinet, awkwardly, while words
dart across, over her head, straight to the father.

A slowly punishable offence she commits
without knowing, within this unidentifiable shell

called 'woman', on infertile land, nameless, label-less,
without a shared anecdotal history of sleepless nights

and hours in A&E. Words skim over her silhouette,
marking her out like a typo error.

A Stanza to Celebrate Stepchildren

Those fluttering pink heart emojis.
'Lots of love' at the end of a call.
A roast dinner cooked with love.
A little potted rose in a milk jug.

Leaving

Mortgage – his
Bills – hers

Telly – his
Sofa- hers

Jacob's crackers – his
Pistachios – hers

Sports bottle – his
Flask – hers

Star Wars – his
Jane Eyre – hers

Their child…
Their child…

Neither his
nor hers

Reunion

Here we are
just like before -
the sun is on our faces.
We don't brown -

Only burn.

No fence to divide us;
washing hung out to dry;
the shrill voices of our children.
We sit on here in our Friday best
remembering graduations,
Nikah, Decree Nisi.

We fill silences with chit chat
about our kids' puberty, moods,
insecurities, as we sip chai,
wiping swiss roll chocolate
from the corners of our mouths,
laughing 'till we almost cry.

We feel each other's tremors -
our voices quiver and tears with tales
of parallel lives come rolling,
adding salt to our chai.

Longevity

Sometimes, kitchen appliances
outlive the marriage, she thinks,

as she throws in sheets from her new
marriage into her old tumble dryer.

Explosion

Severed limbs, still marked
with honeymoon kisses,
re-attach with rough seams.
She gives herself a new blood supply.

Like a corpse revived,
a post-stroke patient
or a traumatised soldier
she learns to speak and walk again.

Alone

I have myself back: no one owns
my body, my name, my physical freedom,
my thoughts, my peace, my solitude, my dignity.
No longer do I have to: agree, bear, ignore, oblige,
give in, submit, survive. No longer do I have to die.

I'm alone enough, it's quiet enough, to hear my own
heartbeat and the pulse of this new house. For the first time
I have my own toolbox: screwdrivers, nails and screws of every
size.
I take out the stripping knife. After scraping the *s* from *Mrs*
I start working on the myth 'you can't live on your own.'

Shared

My own reflection looks back at me,
pale and tired, beyond which
your boy-becoming-man face
looks at me, slightly embarrassed,
a little concerned.

I'm never so conscious of the tick-tick-tick
of seconds as in this moment,
when the yellow line and the danger
of closing doors divides us.

A thousand thoughts burn my head –
how the pain is the same intensity,
just a different kind of bruise.
Whether you leave or remain,
you die. Either in the rancid cocoon
of a rotting marriage or the hollow haunting
of absence from your child.

Son, you take some of me with you
each time, into the neatly ironed
and folded clothes in your holdall.

And now I've lost you
behind those huddled in the aisle.
Your face is covered by someone's
bag. I fix my eyes on the spot where
I last saw your face. I know exactly

where your scar is – the distance
of four of my fingers behind your ear.

I know the soft hairs on your upper
lip you took scissors to. How we laughed!
I know in a while you'll be thirsty.

The passenger covering your face moves
and you look up at me. Our eyes lock.
I see myself smile with watery eyes.
The whistle blows. The doors close:
theatre curtains come down.
It's the end of the show.

You smile, without blinking
as the coach starts moving
and I walk alongside it,
on the yellow line,
faster and faster,
taking you into my arms with my eyes
until this film reel of tired passengers
clouds my eyes and you're no longer in sight.

In defeat I slow down, standing for a while
on the empty platform, watching the train leave.
An empty crisp packet dances erratically in front of me.

Don't Talk to Strangers

You grow up with this mantra,
yet one day you find yourself

confiding in, disclosing and venting
to a complete stranger on the train.

And it feels good.

IV

Soil of saffron

Widow

I am painting the hands of a widow -
leafy and paisley windows.

Orange permeates as the henna dries
on her shrivelled skin, that was soft long ago.

Soon I reach her fingertips.
She smiles and laughs with us girls.

The moon grins through the cold window,
lighting up the patio.

Munching popcorn and Doritos, I gaze at her perfect
disposition dressed in crisp white clothes:

> *'You are a garment for him*
> *and he is a garment for you'*

Where is her garment?

For the first time I see a woman, not a widow.
She giggles at our jokes and passes more Doritos.

At 9 p.m. our mobiles warm with texts from the mosque
but her phone is quiet while she sits on the prayer mat

with her hennaed hands cupped like an old bride's.
She turns to look at us, with a rehearsed smile,

practiced since the day
her husband died.

Graveyard of Jahelia

~ burial ground for female children in pre-Islamic times ~

Born into the wrong gender,
believed to bring poverty and burden

she was carried in her father's
trembling arms.

He lowered her gently, while she kicked
and giggled, into her freshly dug grave.

He began to throw soil onto her,
handful at a time, and even then she laughed,

anticipating play. Slowly, she began to choke
and suffocate, as her mouth filled with soil.

She didn't have a moment to cry. Now she knew
this wasn't play. She soon lost her breath

when tearful angels took her soul.
She looked down at her father

whilst in the arms of the angels.
She reached out for him, kicking her legs,

but he couldn't hear, so she cried
and cried just as she would

before, but this time
her father didn't run to her.

Instead, with shoulders drooped,
wiping his face, he walked away.

Pilgrimage

The Clock Tower
is a cheap ornament,
the plastic kind that sits on nearly
every aunty's mantelpiece, collecting dust.
Crudely designed, it still seems to pull a crowd,
almost like a place of worship, but not quite.

They talk about how it used to be:
none of this was here, nor this, nor that.
I could be in Dubai, or New York when standing
with my back to the Kaaba. I could be anywhere.

It makes me wish I was here five hundred years ago,
when the walk between Safa and Marwa didn't feel
like dodging sales victims in the Trafford Centre.
I find the rock, all glazed and frozen in time,
where Hajra walked and ran in the heat for water.

I wish I was here just fifty years ago,
so I could see the remaining few bricks from the house
where the prophet Mohammad (peace be upon him)
lived with his wife Khadija. Now that place is a toilet block.

The cranes are taller than the Kaaba.
The place is an industrial site, expanding each day.
The Kaaba is shrinking. There are imitations
of the west – KFC, greasy eateries,
Starbucks, pizzerias and convenient coffee.

The Kaaba is the object in selfies, with prolonged
standing and huddling together of groups,
glowing with pride. Some frustrated pilgrims deeply
absorbed in prayer, frown and shake their heads.

We could be at the Colosseum,
the Empire State Building,
or the Eiffel Tower.

Envying Innocence.

I see the contour of a tiny human,
wrapped loosely in ihram,
on the shoulders of his father,
the mild breeze playing with his golden hair.

His eyes are fixed on the sea of colours
around him: the Indonesian group
in blue headscarves, the Somalis in green,
the Turks in yellow.

His bare shoulders move in unison
and rhythm with his father's footsteps.

Suddenly, I'm aware of my wrongs,
regrets and flaws, my lost years,
my cracked heart, my inability to forgive,
my bitter blood.

Beside Him

Taken from Surah Rehman (verse from Quran)

I

'Two gardens
with spreading branches.
In them will be
two springs flowing.
In them will be
every kind of fruit in pairs,
couches lined with silk brocade
and the fruits of the two gardens
will be near at hand.

There they are, majestic, slender,
of modest gaze - beauties not of this world,
whom neither man nor jinn have touched.
They are like rubies and coral.

There are two other gardens -
dark green in colour.
In them will be two springs
gushing forth water'.

II

She is the one with modest gaze.
She is the ruby and coral of this earth,
beauty of no other world:

her unkept hair, eyes as hollow and dark as mine pits,
that await his return every night,

in their two bed terrace, in the frustrated clatter
of pots and pans, in the silence of distance,
in the pain of swollen feet that carry the weight
of their first unborn.

She is the one with modest gaze.
She is the ruby and coral of this earth,
beauty of no other world.

The Last Prayer

After the warning is signalled
by the horn, the earth and sky will shatter.

If my book of good is heavier on the scales
and I cross the bridge of fine thread,
I will ascend to the gates of the first heaven.

When they offer me fruits in pairs
and garments of green silk, or ask me to taste
from the canals of honey and milk,

      I will refuse,

and wait patiently, barefoot, on the soil of saffron
and pebbles of pearls and rubies – just there,

      by the gate, for you.

The First Time I Saw My Father Cry

It's a blue memory
with blue and red stripes
along the edges.

The edges you tear
as I stand in the doorway
to our living room,
looking up at you stood
in the middle of the room,
in front of that old electric fire.

Maybe I have a hand
on the door frame
or maybe I'm holding a toy.
I don't remember

but this I remember:
being transfixed, a little scared,
worried too, to see tears in your eyes;
the airmail letter being ripped open,
your hands shaking a little.

Your voice is strangely loud and hoarse
and is coming from somewhere else -
a place I don't recognise.

Mum holds you.

Your mother has died.
You're holding the letter tight
as if *she* were her in your hands,
with her head in your lap,
taking her last breaths.

The red and blue stripes
are crumpled.

Farewell Prayers

⁓ In memory of my father. May he rest in peace. Ameen ⁓

When I want to see you I look at my hands and my ankles -
the same bony things I hated all my life, I now love.
There's more of you in me, the frown, the fragile wrists,
the thin calves, the shape of the knee,
the abundant heart that also slams shut.

I hear you in the silence, the sniffles
and shuffles in the room.
I see you in my mother's brow,
her eyes, her sadness, her fingers rolling prayer beads.
I see you on every page of the Quran
we're now together reciting.

You're in the sun lowering itself to sleep,
You're in your teacup I'm drinking from.
You're even in the kitchen:
hospital appointments marked
on the calendar, now obsolete.

Turmeric

*~ In memory of my sister-in-law. May she rest in peace.
Ameen ~*

The little loops in your Rs
make me smile
as I skim labels on jars
in your cupboard:

'Garam Masala'
'Meat Tenderiser'

You, rushing about from cooker
to sink, from cupboard to table.
Neglected peels on a newspaper.
The smells of new recipes,
unknown flavours, bottles of fizz,
steam on the window.

That old tea towel with fading herbs.
Hot ladles of chatter warming our plates
as the sun closes its eyes.

I turn one jar of turmeric
to see the whole label,
yellowed by the rush
of your fingertips.
I see jaundice in your eyes.

Touching the label
I think of your gravestone,
then holding the jar, your coffin.

As if in mid-chore, while stirring,
you went to answer the phone
but forgot to come back;
as if these jars are waiting
for your return.

Birthday Reminder

I wake up and slide my finger
to the right on the screen,
accidentally, still comatose from a dream.

I see the annual reminder which I set
five years ago, of your birthday.
A week before, to buy you a card,

a present maybe. My finger freezes
just as it did when you crushed
my hand for comfort.

I sit up, fully awake, in the chaos
of morphine, the dark scent of Black Seed oil,
monitor beeps and your shrinking face,

the mark of your wedding band on your bare finger,
the slow thump and thud of every second,
the agony in which you tossed and turned.

I close my phone with a sharp click
without deleting the reminder
that this is a temporary existence.

Officer

Crickets are still dancing.
Solar lights fixed deep
in dry earth, maintain some life
around his house.

Half drawn curtains
reveal white sheets:
the shrouds for furniture,
stacked against the glass.
The window looks streaked with grief.

You tell me that they had fought
just before he left.
An hour later he crashed.
When they unzipped his body bag,
she collapsed at his broken legs.

The trees are trembling now.
Another storm is near.
We say a *dua* at the gate.
I almost hear the lost sounds
of his children's cheer.

dua: prayer

Father in Gaza

Your home to which you return
Is now a tower block of blown-out

eye sockets, nightmarish, stooping
over the vast field of concrete,

bleeding the voices of children.
Children, who once held these hands.

Hands, now clearing rubble, brick, bone,
teeth and toys. Dolls with missing limbs,

and bullet –holed belly buttons,
their faces grey with grime, dust, ash and blood.

A father rescues a doll's face to reveal
a plastic smile mimicking his own.

Cordoba

Castle-fort-cathedral-mosque hybrid,
decaying but standing, like an old man
weak from life, bells and mimbars,
crosses and 'Ya Allah, Ya Mohammad' side by side.

The silhouettes of tourists inside, by the cutwork window
are indistinguishable. Everyone looks the same.
Mecca and Rome. A healing wound that's
freshly stitched. The light from a stained glass window
splits into a rainbow on a spot of ground,
where I position myself. It pulls all my elements together.
As oxymoronic as Christianity and Islam side by side,
I co-exist with myself as much as with my neighbour.

I sit under the light shining from the stained glass window –
my cheek is orange, my head is yellow, with a violet mouth
I ask the walls: *which of us is whole? Which of us is singular?*

V

Making stars out of shards

Acceptance

Don't let yourself be pulled through hoops of fire
only to be handed a medal of bronze, not gold.

Animosity

Never to speak when alive
but to be present at the funeral,
(of course) whoever goes first.

Beauty

'You're even more beautiful now,
with silver in your hair.'

What is *grey* to one is *shimmering* to another.

Creativity

Is not something in you and not in me,
or something in me and not in you.
We all have it; we don't all know.

Culture

It can be
music, dance, art or poetry.

It can be
the invisible loose noose around your neck.

Displacement

Change it to *perfectly displaced*
by thinking that from this grim
city you can travel
to pretty much anywhere.

Favouritism

The Golden Child knows not
what the copper child feels.

Forgiveness

There is a greater crime
than committing one –
to never forgive one another.

Intelligence

The artist child will always live
in the shadow of the scientist child.

Kindness

Everyone has fire in them:
push their kindness to the limit
and even that will kindle into a storm.

Labelling

Grading starts not from the first day of school
but from the day that the camera peeps into the womb.

Loneliness and Solitude

Do not confuse solitude with loneliness
and if you're lonely, look for solitude within that.

To be lonely is to die a little each day.
To be solitary is to live a little.

Perspective

Some people see dots.
Others see lines.
The rest see circles.

Stubbornness

Can make you close doors upon yourself,
only to later open better ones.

Success

We measure by occupation,
the tax bracket,
the branding of clothes,
the size of the mansion,
the car (s) on the drive,
the number of cleaners,
holidays per year.

Of course, the rest of
us are all failures.

Value

Respond from the position you're given.
No matter how hard you try,
no matter how little you try,
some people will see you only
through the lens they choose.

Illustration acknowledgements

Korinoxe, page 9
Stepanenko Oksana, page 37
Chotwitnote, page 59
Kateryna Vlasenko, page 99
Cover design, night sky by DAPA Images

Lightning Source UK Ltd.
Milton Keynes UK
UKHW010648151021
392221UK00002B/4/J